THE LAST OF THE MARX BROTHERS' WRITERS

Louis Phillips

BROADWAY PLAY PUBLISHING INC
New York
www.broadwayplaypublishing.com
info@broadwayplaypublishing.com

THE LAST OF THE MARX BROTHERS' WRITERS
© Copyright 2007 Louis Phillips

First printing: October 2007
I S B N: 978-0-88145-339-3

Book design: Marie Donovan
Word processing: Microsoft Word
Typographic controls: Ventura Publisher
Typeface: Palatino
Printed and bound in the U S A

THE LAST OF THE MARX BROTHERS' WRITERS
was first produced at the Old Globe Theater, San Diego.
October 1977. The cast was:

JIMMY BRYCE	Victor Buono
JULIUS DUMONT	Sandy McCallum
ALICE UPJOHN MACLOY	Carole Marget
BELLHOP	Lart Ohlson
FRANK CLANDENBERG	Edwin Kotula
Director	Craig Noel

The play was subsequently produced at the Solari
Theater, Beverly Hills, in January 1978. The cast was:

JIMMY BRYCE	Victor Buono
JULIUS DUMONT	Sandy McCallum
ALICE UPJOHN MACLOY	Carole Marget
BELLHOP	William Halliday
FRANK CLANDENBERG	Tris Solari
Director	Rudi Solari

dedicated to the late
Victor Buono
who so magnificently brougt Jimmy Bryce
to life

ACT ONE

*(The scene is a room in a run-down hotel in Los Angeles.
JIMMY BRYCE lies in his lied, surrounded by a stack of
newspapers. The floor around the bed is littered with
newspapers, bottles, laundry, cigarette butts, etc.
Next to the bed is a nightstand with a telephone.
A floor lamp with a discolored lampshade flanks the
nightstand. Upstage is a makeshift wooden closet and
two large windows. A seventeen-inch television set upon
a metal stand is at the foot of the bed. The other furniture in
the room invades a dresser and bureau.)*

*(At the cue of the curtain, BRYCE sits in bed. reading the
papers, smoking a cigarette, and half-listening to a daytime
television program. From outside the windows, we can hear
the sounds of traffic. but BRYCE pays no attention. From time
to time, BRYCE indulges in a fit of coughing and takes some
medicine from his night table-some foul tasting care-all.
On the floor by the bed is a battered portable typewriter
with a sheet of old yellow paper in it.)*

*(BRYCE is a large man, overweight, and in his sixties.
His hair is thinning and soon be will be bald.)*

BRYCE: *(To the audience.)* I know what you're thinking.
Soon I'm going to be bald. Hah, hah, well I'm not....
O K, so I'm going to be, but what's that to you? That's
why I stay in bed all day-so that if my hair falls out,
I'll know where it is. It's going to be right here in bed
with me. I wake up in the morning, grab a handful of
my hair, and toss it over my head. I always shower with

my hair in the morning. Don't you wish everybody
did? *(He crawls down to the edge of the bed and turns down
the television set.)* I don't know why I don't get one of
those remote control units, so I don't have to crawl
from one end of the bed to the other just to change
the channels...I keep saying to myself: Jimmy Bryce,
old boy...Jimmy Bryce, you might have heard of me.
I used to write some of the gags for the Marx Brothers'
comedies. *Horsefeathers. Night at the Opera, A Day at
the Circus, A Day and A Night at the Circus Opera with
Horsefeathers*...I worked them all. Did all their funniest
bits. Naaah. What am I thinking of? You've never heard
of me. You guys don't read credits. It's the title and
the stars, that's all you ever look at. Of course, I didn't
always write under my real name. I used Dostoyevski
a lot, and that might also fool you... After all, I don't
expect you to know everything.... But I'll never forget....
Harpo came up to me one time and told me that the
Marx Brothers would be nothing without me. Nothing.
He took that horn of his and went BEEP, BEEP, BEEP,
BEEP—I mean when you see Harpo honking away in
the movies that's what he's saying— "Jimmy Bryce,
the Marx Brothers would be nowhere without you."
(He crawls back beneath the covers.) But anyway, I keep
saying to myself— "Jimmy Bryce, if you had one of
those remote control clickers, You could sit back in
bed and change the channels, like a pascha, a sultan,
insultin a Sultan... You wouldn't have to crawl back and
forth like some miserable slave." *(He takes up a paper and
fans himself.)* Could use some air-conditioning in this
hotel. Air conditioning, that's what I could use. But
who can afford it nowadays? I hardly have enough
money to get buried with... Besides if everyone runs
his air-conditioning at the same time, all the electricity
will go off. Brown-outs, blackouts, pink-outs. The way
I look at it is that it's my civil duty to sit here in my
undershorts and sweat like a pig.

(The phone rings. BRYCE *starts to answer it immediately, but be controls himself. He waits, then answers it, faking a feminine voice.)*

BRYCE: The Beverly Wilshire. Mister Jimmy Bryce... Just a minute. I'll ring his suite for you. *(His voice back to normal)* Yeah, who is it? Herby Feingold? Who are you?... Oh, you're a friend of my agent... good for you... What agent? ...Gold, Bucks, and Rose Agency? ...I thought those guys died a long time ago... What did they do, lose my phone number? No, of course not. They gave it to you. For a moment I thought you saw it scribbled on a bathroom wall.... Yeah, I'm a great kidder. Groucho got it all from me... Look, tell me, who are you a friend of? Gold, Bucks, or that Rose? ...Rose... Imagine naming a kid Rose... No wonder he became an agent. Who's he representing now, now that he's got all that free time on his hands? Last I heard from him he was handling Vennevecchi and Bilbo and their dancing owl... What do you mean what free time? I haven't heard from those guys in six years, and now they're handing out my phone number like M & Ms... What is this —National Resurrect a Schmuck Week? ...Oh, they told you I was a great gag writer, did they? How do they know? They can't even read. Rose moves his lips and Bucks stares at the walls...I'd send them over my simplest gags, and you'd think I was writing a Papal Encyclical... E as in Emory, N as in Nuptial Bliss, C as in... Forget it... What do you want? Yeah, that's right I used to write for the Marx Brothers. Groucho, Chico, Harpo, Gummo, Zeppo, and Flammo. Plammo? What do you mean you never heard of Flammo. He was the sixth of the Brothers, but the editors kept cutting him out. That's right. Flammo. I was the face on the cutting room floor...I even wrote the honks for Harpo's horn. You think be thought those honks up all by himself? He didn't know a harp from a kazoo until I showed him... Of course they were very funny honks... Of course, I'm the guy you're looking for... Of course, it depends what you're looking for, lover lips... *(He breaks into a spell of severe coughing. He grabs for the bottle of medicine upon his night table and takes a swig.)* No. It's nothing. I'll be all right... Excuse me...I'll be O K, it's just that the air-conditioning's up too high... *(Calls out to his invisible servant)* Mathilde, will you turn down the air-conditioning here? Here comes Nanook and his dog sled now. *(Barks into the phone)* Just a cough. My doctor, you know the one who does the heart transplants? ...He wants me to go to Palm Springs, but I was afraid I'd miss a call from my agents. Six years I've been waiting. I think the last time I heard from them was when I optioned a script to Rin Tin Tin... Whatja say their names are again? That's right. Gold, Bucks, and Rose... Yeah, I'm a great kidder... Don't tell me. Tell it to the Academy Awards people. You see the junk they nominated this time? *(He sits on the edge of the bed, opens a drawer in the night table, removes a bottle of vodka, and finishes it.)* Look, I'm a busy man. I don't feel like talking to you about the rotten Academy Awards. If this were a friendly call, I would have called you... Besides you've got to write serious stuff to get an award. You don't think people take a thing like *Duck Soup* seriously do you? Christ. People don't want movies anymore. They want flagellation. You go in with popcorn and you come out with a social conscience...I know one movie where they've built a ticket booth out front and a confessional booth in the rear... The last movie I saw made me so unhappy I wanted to kill myself. So what happened? The critics gave it their circular prize, or whatever the hell it was... All right, why don't you shut up so I can listen... Are you sure you didn't want the number for Dial-a-Resurrection and ended up with me? *(He lies back with the phone to his ear and begins rummaging through the newspapers. He kicks a few pages to the floor, balances the magazine section on his toes.)* Yes, for

Chrissakes, I'm listening. You represent this young
punk, and he wants to write comedy... Don't they all...
Tell him to go into politics... That's where all the big
laughs are

(Noise from the street)

BRYCE: Look, pay no attention to the noise...It's just
some dwarves left over from an old Walt Disney set.
They always come in this time of day to clean up...
Doc, stop doing that to Dopey...

*(Out from under BRYCE's bed pokes the head of JULIUS
DUMONT, whose appearance may or may not resemble
anybody in particular. He has a moustache and a cigar
in his mouth.)*

BRYCE: How old's your client? What difference does it
make? I just want to make sure that we're not involved
with any child prodigy. Child prodigies are murder.
A child prodigy is the one thing Nature abhors more
than a vacuum... He's nineteen and he's working on
this script... What the hell is a nineteen-year-old kid
doing with a script? Hasn't he got anything better to
do with his time.... So what if I was writing for the Marx
Brothers when I was twenty-two. Twenty-two is not
nineteen. There's a world of difference.... Look, I'm
three times older than the kid, and I've got a trunk load
of scripts. Why don't you take some of mine. I've got
one here that Doris Day liked almost... You want me
to teach this kid everything I know?
    What's he going to pay me?
    Fifteen dollars an hour? Where's a kid of nineteen
getting that kind of money... Oh, he's already sold a
script already... Look, I'm a writer myself. I ain't no
teacher... What do you want me to do, take the best
gags right out of the heart of my scripts and hand them
over to some punk for fifteen dollars an hour... You
must be kidding. When I get something good, I use it
myself... What's it to you the last time I sold anything...

What do you think? Think you can learn comedy? It's a gift from God... You expect me to sweat all my life to hand it over to some punk?... He wants to meet with me for lunch or something... Well, it's a nice thought... No, no, I can't leave my room...I haven't been outside in six years...I'm allergic to alienation... Look, do yourself a favor, I have a lot of good material, why don't you buy it from me... O K, its your loss... Maybe I'll hold an auction for sight gags and one-liners... What do I hear for this titter? Belly-laughs are more expensive...I'll tell you what, just leave his name and number and maybe I'll give him a call... Then maybe again maybe I won't...

(Looking for a pencil. JULIUS *hands him one. A giant one)*

BRYCE: After all there's lots of comedy schools around. P S 93. The Albert Schweitzer memorial school of comedy... That's the kid's name, huh. Frank Clandenberg. Is that with two clandens? With a name like that he's gonna get laughs...554-6782.... He thought he'd come right over to the Beverly Wilshire and look me up...don't do that...I'm not going to work at home... The air-conditioning's too cold... I'll get a room somewhere.... But I'm not sure I want to do it...I don't have anything to teach anybody.... Look, if he don't hear from me by the time of the Third World War, then tell him to try somebody else. The world is full of gag men. Just turn on the C B S Evening News... Yeah, don't mention it... Hey if you see Gold, Bucks, or Rose...If you see any of those guys, tell them I say hello. *(He hangs up. Thinks better of it, picks up phone quickly)* No, tell them to shove it... *(He hangs up.)* Imagine the gall of those guys. Ignore me for six years so they figure I want to sell my stuff to some nineteen-year-old punk, they think I want to open up a school of comedy...I am a school... *(Calls for* JULIUS*)* Julius!

JULIUS: *(Stands up, brushes himself off)* .1 wish you'd vacuum under the bed once in a while...I'd like to give

up lint for Lent...for Arthur Lunt. Lint for Lent for Lunt.
Sounds like a double play combination for the Chicago
Cubs. But then everything sounds like a double-play
combination for the Chicago Cubs. Brinks to Banks to
Bunks.

BRYCE: Julius Dumont.

JULIUS: I prefer to be called Flammo.

BRYCE: Go away—I made him up.

JULIUS: Its a lie. It's worse than a lie. It's also worse than
a lay now that I think of it. The trouble with you, Bryce,
is that you forget you're a liar... *(He pecks at* BRYCE's
battered typewriter.) ...The worst liar who ever lived.
Not counting the great writers of course. Homer,
Shakespeare, Mother Goose. Now there's lying for you.
Writing about Helen and Cleopatra and Lady Godiva.
Now there's laying for you. Mother Goose. What a way
to treat your mother.

BRYCE: *(Impatiently.)* Cut it out, Flammo, will ya? *(He
has another attack of coughing.)* Can't you see I'm dying?

(He reaches for the bottle of vodka, but JULIUS *takes it and
tastes it for himself.)*

JULIUS: Hold it...It's O K. Go ahead...

BRYCE: I'm shaking.

JULIUS: So what? Didn't D W Griffith die right in this
hotel, right next door practically? Are you better than
D W Griffith? For crying our loud, nobody's better than
D W Griffith...

BRYCE: Are you going to do Groucho forever?

JULIUS: *(Removing his glasses)* Forever? Nothing is
forever... Some flies live only one day, they buzz and
they die, and they don't even laugh... *(Resumes disguise)*
And when are you going to get air-conditioning in this
hell hole? You're just doing this to discourage me from

visiting... (*Picks up the phone*) Hello, Room Service, send up a bucket of cold air... Send up a room... Send us something to confirm our existence!

BRYCE: While you're at it, have them send up a priest. I'm dying.

JULIUS: What do you want a priest for? You're not Catholic.

BRYCE: I don't want a rabbi to have to climb five flights of stairs.

JULIUS: How can you die when this is Marx Brothers week on Channel 5 and they're showing *The Big Store* at three?

BRYCE: (*Suddenly rejuvenated. He gets out of bed, takes a piece of chalk, and makes a mark on a wall that is, covered with chalk marks. He makes a rapid count,*) One hundred and ten, one hundred and eleven, one hundred and twelve. That's it. This will be the one hundred and twelfth time I've sat through a Marx Brothers comedy... *Big Store*... Some good routines in that film... Douglas Dumbrille plays the villain, doesn't he? (*Quotes a line from the film*) "Bloodhounds transfused-fingerprints manicured-Gin Rummy." (*Glances at all the scripts piled in the corner.*) Look at all those scripts. I haven't sold a script, a gag, a quip, in sixteen years, and everybody's going around quoting the old jokes...It's getting so people only laugh in retrospect...

JULIUS: (*Takes out three giant envelopes from beneath the bed*) Here's your mail. There ought to be lots of laughs in that. The one on top's from Boys Town.

BRYCE: Boys Town. I really ought to write them some day. (*Looks at the number of his room.*) I owe them about five hundred and seventy-six letters.

JULIUS: The telephone company's writing again. Threatening to turn off your phone if you don't pay.

BRYCE: Why don't they just call me?

JULIUS: They've tried, but their dime keeps coming back.

BRYCE: *(Holds a letter up to the light.)* What's this?
...This is the letter I wrote to Donald MacBride.
It's come back.... You remember. Donald MacBride.
Made his screen debut in *Room Service*... Now there
is a funny man for you.

JULIUS: Dead.

BRYCE: Dead? Now there *was* a funny man.

JULIUS: This is 1978 for Chrissakes. They're all dead.
MacBride. Arthur.

BRYCE: Arthur too? ...Where have I been the last sixteen
years. *(He tosses the letter out the window.)* I've become
the Rip Van Winkle of the Down and Out Set... Arthur
and MacBride. *(Angrily)* I bet there isn't even a Boys
Town anymore. It's been dismantled, taken down.

JULIUS: What's the date on that letter?

BRYCE: *(Calls out the window)* What's the date on that
letter?

VOICE: *(From the street below)* What?

BRYCE: I bet I've been throwing out that letter for
sixteen years. That same letter, and somebody's
been picking it out of the trash cans, stuffing it in
an envelope, and mailing it back to me.

JULIUS: *(Standing on the bed.)* Look, don't go bananas
on me... All right, go bananas—it's cheaper than flying.
Besides, who ever dies in a banana crash. I had an uncle
once who died in the market crash, had stock in
bananas and then it split. We had banana splits ever
since...

BRYCE: God, I've got to have some human contact.

JULIUS: Don't settle for second best.

BRYCE: Even if it is some punk... What did I do with that number?

JULIUS: Maybe it wasn't in bananas. Maybe he was in mustard. But then who ever heard of a mustard split... *(Tosses his banana peel out the window)* What are you looking for?

BRYCE: *(Looking through the newspapers)* Clandenberg's number.

JULIUS: Why didn't you write it down? *(He starts taking out all the dresser drawers, searching for the number.)*

BRYCE: I did write it down. It was on a small piece of paper. Maybe 1 put it on the back of my prescription.

JULIUS: What did the number look like?

BRYCE: What do you mean, what did it look like? How can a number look like anything? A number is unique. Sixty-nine is sixty-nine. Eight-seven is eighty-seven. In the entire world there is only one thirty-eight.

JULIUS: Hike...I've seen a lot of girls with thirty-eights... Don't give me this individualist stuff... You've seen one number and you've seen them all.

BRYCE: Look, you're making a mess. Every time you come in here, you make a mess.

JULIUS: If you think this is a mess, you should have seen your act in Omaha...

BRYCE: Quiet! I got it. 554-6782. *(He dials the number.)* I'm going to ask him to come up. I need somebody to talk to and I can use the money...I need something to be buried with... There aren't going to be any guys running around the office taking up a collection for me...

JULIUS: Won't Heaven take souls on credit?

BRYCE: Mmm-Mmm.

*(During the following, BRYCE talks to FRANK
CLANDENBERG on the phone, inviting the kid to come up to
the hotel room. BRYCE talks but we don't bear what be says.
He is obviously explaining that he has rented a room for
them to work in and is giving the kid directions.)*

JULIUS: Tell him we want the cash up front. We're not
proud. We'll take it up back too.

*(ALICE UPJOHN MACLOY crawls in through the window.
She will be various ages in different scenes, but now she is
in her forties, not exactly unpretty, and slightly unsteady
on her feet. The crawl up the side of the building and through
the window has her worn out. On top of her bat is the banana
peel Julius had discarded.)*

ALICE: *(To JULIUS.)* You're giving up, aren't you?

(JULIUS shrugs his shoulders.)

ALICE: You're going to give all those beautiful scripts
away...

JULIUS: What are you going to do? You can't take them
with you.

ALICE: That's the trouble with you, you big lug.
Every time you got something good, you give it
away—for peanuts. You write a funny line, and in
it goes into someone else's head and out it comes
from somebody else's mouth. You never learn to keep
anything for yourself.

BRYCE: *(His hand over the receiver)* Quiet. Can't you see
I'm on the phone?

JULIUS: It's all in the timing.

BRYCE: *(Looks thoughtful)* Kid, It's all in the timing.

ALICE: Sure. You have to have timing, but first you've
got to have good lines...

BRYCE: *(Hangs up.)* The kid is on his way up.

ALICE: And what's he gonna pay you I remember when you were sending in gags to the Fred Allen Show for free. That's you, Jim-Jim, always afraid of a little success...

BRYCE: *(Standing on the bed and wrapping the sheets about him)* I write the lines. I don't deliver.

ALICE: Story of your life, ain't it?

BRYCE: I wrote routines for the Marx Brothers.

ALICE: And you got that all by yourself, didn't you

(BRYCE glances at her with a hurt expression. JULIUS reappears as Harpo and wipes a tear from BRYCE's eye.)

ALICE: Ah, Jim-Jim, I didn't mean it... The climb up the side of the building makes me cranky. You know me, honey... It seems to me, the least an ex-husband can do is live on the ground floor.

(JULIUS takes a red wig out of one of the bureau drawers and tosses it to BRYCE. BRYCE puts it on. ALICE opens up the large knit bag she is carrying and takes out a cactus and places it on the dresser.)

BRYCE: *(Getting into the wig)* What's that?

ALICE: It's no bowling ball.

BRYCE: What do I want with a cactus?

ALICE: It ain't no big responsibility. For Chrissakes, you don't even have to water it.

BRYCE: *(Getting into white pants and a white shirt.)* Water? Who's talking about water? I'm talking about photosynthesis. Now I'm going to be up all night worrying about chlorophyll.

(JULIUS takes off his glasses, opens the closet, where a myriad of objects come tumbling out-strange props from a bygone era, along with pots. pans, bottles. There are quite a few empty flower pots.)

ALICE: Whoever heard of worrying about photochlorophyll? You must be getting ready for the loony bin.

BRYCE: I didn't invent the universe. That plant is going to take oxygen from the air. How am I going to breathe? ...Its getting harder for me to breathe already.

ALICE: You live in Los Angeles, don't you? Nobody breathes in Los Angeles. As usual, you got it all backwards. Even your science is out of date. Take my advice, Jim-Jim, and don't let Clandenbuttocks come up here... Your material is good when it comes from you, you just can't hand it over... It's yours and it's worth something...

BRYCE: My jokes are coming back as nostalgia.

ALICE: Then let the producers buy your scripts as mementos, and make your fortune...

JULIUS: *(From the closet.)* Quiet on the set...

(BRYCE *takes out a clapboard. The abbreviation "mos" and the year "1933" are chalked upon it.)*

BRYCE: Scene one, take one.

ALICE: You just won't understand each other.

JULIUS: Mid out sound.

BRYCE: I have this idea for a new movie—*The Giant Sponge Soaks Up Chicago.* You cross a camel with a cactus, and you get-in addition to a very cross camel—this thing, animal-vegetable, call it a prickly camel, and it's gone without water for about sixteen years. It flies through outer space until it lands in Detroit.

ALICE: Omaha. Detroit doesn't get laughs.

BRYCE: Kissimee.

ALICE: You never know where you are.

BRYCE: Soon the entire population of Omaha-Detroit falls down and worships this monument to thirst because there isn't any water left in the world. General Motors has polluted everything out of existence.

ALICE: I've got the ending. It falls in love with a cow and gives birth to powdered milk.

BRYCE: Why do you always do that to me?

ALICE: Look, you're a gag writer. Cut out the social commentary. What's all this about General Motors drying everything up? You want to get slapped with a lawsuit? You'll be in court until hell freezes over.

BRYCE: How can hell freeze over if there's no water left?

ALICE: There's a lot of moisture present in the memory. You see the universe has a memory and it retains every drip, drop, and droop.

BRYCE: Ah, you read that somewhere.

ALICE: Yeah, you know me. I ain't got no brains of my own.

BRYCE: I didn't mean that.

ALICE: Yes, you do. Didn't I go bananas on you? ...I was the charm and you were the brains...1933 and we were going places together....

(JULIUS *comes out of the closet with director's chair, dark glasses and wearing a beret. He carries a horse whip.*)

JULIUS: *(Director)* Quiet on the set.

(BRYCE *climbs off the bed and stands next to* ALICE *in front of the director who sits sternly in his chair.* ALICE *shakes out her red hair and pins a silk scarf to the front of her blouse.*)

BRYCE: *(Stage whisper)* I don't understand why you're getting so tense. It's just a crummy screen test.

ALICE: Why do you have to change the material all the time for? I just get one bit down and you're tinkering with it, changing it around, and I've got to do most of the memorizing.

BRYCE: Remembering ain't hard... Damn it, Alice, this is our big chance... We've got to calm down. *(Takes a hip flask out of his back pocket and takes a sip.)*

ALICE: Is that going to help?

JULIUS: *(Director)* Who told you to wear white? Do you know anything about films? White picks up all kinds of glare. It makes it hard for the cameraman to get a reading on you... Don't you have a sweater or something? You look like a walking iceberg.

(BRYCE goes through one of the bureau drawers on the floor and comes up with a moth-eaten odd-colored sweater. He puts it on.)

JULIUS: *(Director)* White! You would think you were virgins or something.

ALICE: *(To lighten the tension)* It's virgin wool.

JULIUS: *(Director)* Hey, that's a hot one... You the brains of this outfit?

ALICE: No, no. My husband here writes all our material.

JULIUS: *(Director)* Look, honey. I don't care if you were Theda Bara and he were Mount Whitney. This test is costing everybody money. Now let's get something down for the studio to look at. I'm a busy man, I ain't got all day. I got a picture to make—roll 'em.

BRYCE: I've seen your last picture so don't go rushing us....

JULIUS: *(Director)* What do you mean by that crack?

ALICE: He didn't mean nothing by it... *(To BRYCE)* Come on, honey, let's do the lost cousin routine...

JULIUS: (Director) Maybe you ought to come down off your high horse, wise guy.

BRYCE: Me come down off my high horse! You're the one trying to rush us so that we flub up... You just don't turn on and off this kind of material like a light switch...I mean we're improvising up here too...

JULIUS: (Director) Well forgive me, your highness... I didn't realize we were handling stuff for the ages up here.

BRYCE: Not stuff for the ages. At least it's not your last film— *Rin-Tin-Tin Sucks Eggs to Save Western Civilization...*

JULIUS: (Director) Cut! Let's call it a wrap, huh. (Getting up from his chair) The girl there (Indicates ALICE.) can stay if she wants...

(BRYCE *falls down to his hands and knees in a ferocious imitation of Rin-Tin-Tin. He bites the* JULIUS *in the ankle.* ALICE *pulls* BRYCE *away.*)

ALICE: (Frightened) Jim-Jim, what are you doing? Stop it!

JULIUS: (Director) Get this mad dog off me. Guards... Guards!

BRYCE: (Rises to his full stature) Don't call Rin-Tin-Tin mad. RinTin-Tin is the sanest animal in the universe.

JULIUS: (Director. Furious) Get off this set at once... You won't work in this studio or any studio as long as I'm in Hollywood.

BRYCE: What's the matter with you? Can't you take a little joke?

JULIUS: (Director) Rabies is no joke....

ALICE: (Appealing to JULIUS [Director]) Please. He didn't mean anything by it... He has a strange sense of humor...

(JULIUS *[Director] walks away, returning the chair and props to the closet.*)

JULIUS: *([Director] crawls under the bed)* When you get rid of that jerk, give me a call, baby.

BRYCE: *(Testing his muscles)* What jerk? I don't have a jerk...

ALICE: Jim-Jim, do you see what you've done?

BRYCE: I wasn't going to stand there while some big-shot pushes us around. Who is he anyway? The ruler of the world?

ALICE: Jimmy, why do you cause so much trouble?

BRYCE: I'm a comic, not a roller-derby man. They want to put everybody on skates and make them skate through life...

ALICE: You would think there would be something in you that would want to succeed. Once you make it then you can tell the director to jump in the lake.

BRYCE: Who writes funnier stuff? Me or Rin-Tin-Tin?

ALICE: So, who eats dog food and who eats steak?

BRYCE: That Rin-Tin-Tin stuff is just a fad. Who's going to remember it a hundred years from now? For Chrissakes he doesn't even answer his fan mail.

ALICE: A hundred years from now you'll be dead and I'll be twenty-nine. *(Laughs)* Jim-Jim, a gag's a gag. It doesn't have any meaning beyond the moment. It's a fly that buzzes and dies.

BRYCE: Then why are Chaplin and Keaton doing the same old gags all the time?

ALICE: They ain't doing Alice and Jimmy Bryce!

BRYCE: Idea for a routine, Alice... There's this famous animal star and he's at home answering his fan mail...

You and I would be the secretaries for this famous parakeet, Perky, and we've got to answer the fan mail. *(Takes out a letter, reads it)* "Dear Perky: I caught your last film where you and that Kraut dog saved Western Civilization. You're so brave and true. Do you think we could make whooppee sometime. Signed, Herbert Hoover. P S: I'm available."

ALICE: We have enough routines

BRYCE: There's never enough routines!

ALICE: But I want to eat. At least you get some meat, even if it's a director's leg... Oh, Jim-Jim, if you'd only grow up...

BRYCE: Next time you bite him too... Nothing like dining out.

ALICE: I don't do imitations...

BRYCE: Alice, honey, why don't you imitate a woman for me once in a while?

ALICE: *(Stung)* What do you mean by that, huh?

(There's knocking at BRYCE's hotel door....)

BRYCE: Look, Alice, I'm sorry.

ALICE: I don't like to make love all the time

(ALICE disappears behind screen.... BRYCE knocks on dresser.)

BRYCE: Forget it. I didn't mean anything.

ALICE: No, you never mean anything. It's just one big joke to you.

(Another knock at the door)

BRYCE: Forget it!

ALICE: A minute ago you were yelling at me to remember.

(BELLHOP opens the door slightly.)

BRYCE: *(Loudly)* Forget it!

BELLHOP: O K.

BRYCE: Hey, where are you going with my breakfast"

BELLHOP: You said to forget it.

BRYCE: I wasn't talking to you.

BELLHOP: I thought you were talking to me....
(Enters with breakfast tray)

BRYCE: I've had my breakfast here every morning for the past sixteen years. Why should this morning be different?

BELLHOP: *(Steps cautiously around the newspaper and the bureau drawer)* Maybe you're getting tired of oatmeal.

BRYCE: A comedian. They all think they're comedians....
You new here? I haven't seen you around.

BELLHOP: Started yesterday.

BRYCE: I wrote routines for the Marx Brothers.

BELLHOP: Yeah. The manager told me.

BRYCE: What else did Bernie tell you about me?

BELLHOP: Not much.

BRYCE: You want to see the clippings?

BELLHOP: Look, mister, I only deliver the oatmeal. Maybe some other time, huh?

BRYCE: *(Looking for his scrapbook)* You think maybe I went to some amusement park and had some guy make them up?

BELLHOP: I believe...I just don't think the Marx Brothers are very funny. They never made any sense to me.

BRYCE: They never made any sense to you?

BELLHOP: No.

BRYCE: And they were never very funny.

BELLHOP: No.

BRYCE: What the hell's the matter with you? You an atheist or something?

BELLHOP: There are no atheists in the elevators of this hotel...I just don't think the kind of stuff they did was very funny.

BRYCE: You don't, huh.

BELLHOP: Uh-uh.

BRYCE: Here. Hold this.

(He thrusts a large book into the BELLHOP's bands. During the following. the BELLHOP stands around bewildered, allowing BRYCE to move him about like a prop. BRYCE takes an old Pepsi bottle from his dresser, then picks up a battered canoe paddle, and a metal ashtray that is filled with confetti. He lays the Pepsi bottle on the floor, places the canoe paddle see-saw fashion across the bottle. The raised position of the paddle faces the BELLHOP. On the down side, BRYCE places the ashtray filled with confetti. BRYCE carefully positions the BELLHOP so that the large book is directly over the paddle. BRYCE crosses to his umbrella stand [which contains all kinds of strange objects, props used in old acts] and he removes a short sword.)

BRYCE: (Loudly, with a threatening move toward the BELLHOP) Death to the Infidel!

(The BELLHOP is so startled by the attack that he drops the huge book onto the paddle. The confetti is catapulted into the air. BRYCE steps into the scene so that the confetti rains down over him.)

BELLHOP: (No reaction at all) Well, Mister...I better get going...

BRYCE: *(Breathing heavily from the exercise)* My name is Bryce, Jimmy. *(He breaks off and grabs for the bedpost to steady himself He clutches at his heart. He falls to his knees.)*

BELLHOP: Hey, Mister, what's wrong?

BRYCE: Nothing...I'll be all right... *(Coughing)* I'm just not used to that physical stuff...I'm really a deep thinker.

BELLHOP: Want me to get a doctor?

BRYCE: *(Stretches face up on the floor)* No. No doctor... Let me just lie here a bit. The Coast Guard'll come in and get me at high tide.

BELLHOP: I better get somebody.

BRYCE: I have somebody coming...a guy named Clandenberg.... You send him up when he comes.

BELLHOP: Is he a doctor?

BRYCE: A guy named Clandenberg? What else can he be? I'm not going to die until he gets here...I've got a lot to teach him.

BELLHOP: I'm going to have to report this, Mister Bryce. Bernie said that ever since D W Griffith-the owners have been very touchy about guests dying in the rooms. It gives the hotel a bad name.

BRYCE: I'm all right. I wasn't speaking literally about dying. It's only a figure of speech... You ask your girlfriend's father for her hand in marriage. Fine situation you'd be in, if he only gives you her hand.

BELLHOP: I don't have a girlfriend.

BRYCE: *(Defeated)* Ah, well...

BELLHOP: I'll come back later... Just in case.

BRYCE: Look, do me a favor will ya... *(Hands him the prescription)* Get this prescription filled for me, willya? It's for my cough...

BELLHOP: It's going to cost money?

BRYCE: *(Reaches under the chair. He tosses the* BELLHOP *a rubber chicken.)* No, we'll trade a rubber chicken for it... Charge it...

BELLHOP: *(Leaving)* I'll do it when I can.

BRYCE: Listen, don't say nothing about this to Bernie, huh? ...You can't take language literally. It doesn't make any sense that way.

JULIUS: *(From under the bed)* We made a career out of that.

BRYCE: Sure did.

BELLHOP: What?

BRYCE: Forget it.

*(*BELLHOP *exits.)*

JULIUS: *(As Chico)* What's a Jehovah's Witness going to understand about comedy?

BRYCE: He's a bellhop.

JULIUS: Everyday a new religion... What are you lying on the floor for?

BRYCE: I like the view.

JULIUS: Is that right? What do you see?

BRYCE: The ceiling.

JULIUS: Okey dokey, boss, and what do you see from your bed?

BRYCE: The ceiling... But I'm farther away from it on the floor. It provides a different perspective on the meaning of ceilings... You'd be surprised how many people never look at the ceilings until they get on the floor...

VOICE FROM THE WHIRLWIND: Bryce!

*(*JULIUS *dives under the bed.)*

VOICE FROM THE WHIRLWIND: Bryce, gird up thy loins like a man, for I will demand of thee and answer thou me.

BRYCE: Huh?

VOICE FROM THE WHIRLWIND: Where wast thou when I laid the foundations of the earth? Declare, if thou hast understanding.

BRYCE: I'm working on it.

VOICE FROM THE WHIRLWIND: Who hath laid the measures thereof, if thou knowest.

BRYCE: Huh?

VOICE FROM THE WHIRLWIND: Who hath stretched the line upon it?

BRYCE: You're kidding me.

VOICE FROM THE WHIRLWIND: Let's take it from the top...where wast thou when I laid the foundations of the Earth? Declare, if thou has understanding.

BRYCE: Can't I have an expert in the booth with me?

JULIUS: *(Popping his head out from under the bed)* That's me, boss.

VOICE FROM THE WHIRLWIND: Or who shut up the sea with doors?

JULIUS: We've got him now. Who ever heard of the sea shut up with doors? He's crazy.

(JULIUS goes back under the bed)

VOICE FROM THE WHIRLWIND: Where is the way where Light dwelleth?

BRYCE: Why can't I have my oatmeal in peace once in a while,

VOICE FROM THE WHIRLWIND: Hath the rain a feather?

JULIUS: *(Popping out)* Hath the rain a feather?

BRYCE: Whatever he says gets published, gets quoted.

(Two small white feathers fall from the ceiling.)

JULIUS: Why don't you ask who his agent is? I bet it's not Gold, Bucks and Rose.

VOICE FROM THE WHIRLWIND: Wouldst thou fill thy belly with the east wind... What is the capital of Nebraska?

BRYCE: *(Incredulous)* What is the capital of Nebraska?

VOICE FROM THE WHIRLWIND: I asked you first... You weren't doing very well with the other questions. I thought I'd try something else.

BRYCE: The other questions were hard. What do I know from the foundations of the earth? Why don't you ask George S. Kaufman or some of the other writers?

VOICE FROM THE WHIRLWIND: Dead.

BRYCE: All of them?

VOICE FROM THE WHIRLWIND: Most.

BRYCE: George S Kaufman?

VOICE FROM THE WHIRLWIND: Dead.

BRYCE: Oh, why did you go and do that for? A man who's got good gags ought to live forever

(Offstage vaudeville sounds. An announcer introduces Vennevecchi and Bilbo. Lights up on ALICE. She enters from the bathroom dressed in her bathrobe and wig. She angrily removes her wig.)

ALICE: Why did you go and do that for?

BRYCE: *(Stands up, removes his black bow tie)* Do what?

ALICE: *(Looking in the crazy mirrors)* The job routine... Why did you have to do the Job routine?

BRYCE: It's one of my best bits. It keeps them in the aisles.

ALICE: Not in Omaha it don't... *(Turns to face* BRYCE)... Couldn't you see them walking out, clutching their children like bags of groceries under their arms?

BRYCE: I'm not deaf...I know when I'm not getting the laughs.

ALICE: Then whatja do it for? You can't make fun of the Bible in Omaha. Why didn't we do the lost cousin routine?

BRYCE: I figured since Omaha's the capital that we'd have a more sophisticated audience than that.

ALICE: Lincoln's the capital, not Omaha.

BRYCE: Lincoln? Since when?

ALICE: Since always. You see, God created Man, then Woman, and then he reached out and created Lincoln, Nebraska.

BRYCE: No wonder my Job routine didn't work. Omaha isn't the capital.

ALICE: The Civil War had more laughs... Why didn't you cut it short?

BRYCE: What was I going to do? Stop in the middle and apologize? You can't do that! A routine's like a marriage. It's a commitment. It's a gamble. It's a risk— all or nothing. Otherwise you're just a hack.

ALICE: Jim-Jim, just give them the corn. Why did the chicken cross the road?

BRYCE: To prove that he and the road both existed at the same time... Lots of laughs in Iowa...

ALICE: Nebraska. I think you did it on purpose, Jim-Jim.

BRYCE: Did what, Alice-Alice...

ALICE: Choose choose a a wrong wrong routine...I don't know why you do it. Just when things begin to look up for us, you do something to spoil it, like you're trying to fail and fail and fail...

BRYCE: Sure.

ALICE: What do you have against success? A little success wouldn't hurt us.

BRYCE: Success? ...I wouldn't touch it with a ten-foot Pole...a nine-foot Armenian maybe.

ALICE: Can't you see what you're doing to us?

(Knock at door)

BRYCE: I said I'm sorry, didn't I? Everybody has a bad night. If a man got laughs all the time, he'd be a roaring idiot. *(He discovers the cactus upon the dressing table.)* ...What's this? What's this cactus doing here?

ALICE: Somebody sent it backstage to us...a dry sense of humor.

BRYCE: *(Angered by the insult)* Somebody sent us a cactus? Is this their idea of a joke? *(He picks it up and throws it in the wastepaper basket.)* I'll show those local yokels...

ALICE: Jim-Jim, don't...

BRYCE: Don't what?

ALICE: *(Takes the cactus out of the basket, rescues it)* Don't throw it away...I want it.

BRYCE: They insult you and you want to thank them for it?

ALICE: Please, Jim-Jim, let me keep it... it's going to bring us luck...I feel it... Please. *(She places the cactus back upon the dressing table.)*

BRYCE: This life isn't good for you, Alice...I'm going to send my routines to the radio shows...

ALICE: No.

BRYCE: What do you mean no?

ALICE: What do you want to give our good stuff away for?

BRYCE: Fm not giving it away. I'm selling it.

ALICE: Are you kidding? They hear a gag on radio and then it's dead forever. Everybody's heard it, And they won't pay enough. I know you... Every time you come up with something good you just want to hand it over to somebody else...

BRYCE: So, when we're dead, who's going to remember the routines?

ALICE: Who cares after we're dead? You're not writing stuff for the ages... Just make them laugh and get off the stage.

BRYCE: I learned it from somebody...and somebody's going to learn it from me...

ALICE: *(Pours herself a drink from* BRYCE's *flask)* What for? ...The times will be so different then that everybody will have a whole new sense of humor or none at all.

BRYCE: Since when did you start drinking?

ALICE: Since when were you afraid of making people laugh?

BRYCE: It's time to quit or change partners.

(JULIUS *comes riding on stage on a bicycle. The bicycle carries a cardboard sign— "The Great Flammo". * JULIUS *beeps the bicycle horn, bits the bicycle bell.* JULIUS *rides into* BRYCE *and tips over Lights down on* ALICE. *During the following routine, delivered at breakneck pace,* ALICE *climbs* *into bed and pulls the covers over her. The act has the flavor of an English music hall turn.)*

BRYCE: Hi, mate.

JULIUS: I'm new hereabouts.

BRYCE: Hear what bouts?

JULIUS: Why there's a whole flock of bouts. Don't you hear them?

BRYCE: I never heard a bouts.

JULIUS: It's not a herd of bouts. It's a flock of bouts.

BRYCE: Is the flock of bouts hereabouts?

JULIUS: Hear what bouts?

BRYCE: I don't even know what a bouts is. What's a bout?

JULIUS: Got me.

BRYCE: What a bout is is a little furry mammal that flies in the dark.

JULIUS: Whereabout?

BRYCE: No, you can't wear a bouts.

JULIUS: You can't wear a bout hereabouts?

BRYCE: Hear a bouts? I've told you I've never heard a bouts.

JULIUS: Well, is the herd nearabouts?

BRYCE: Near a bouts? You don't want to get near a bouts. In fact, it's better if you don't even know a bout's whereabouts.

JULIUS: I thought you can't wear a bouts.

BRYCE: We've been through that.

JULIUS: I must be getting lost.

BRYCE: That's because you came by such a roundabout way.

JULIUS: Round, a bout?

BRYCE: Well, they're not perfectly round...

JULIUS: Howabout that!

BRYCE: How a bout? Do you mean a roustabout?

JULIUS: Who ever heard of a flock of roustabouts?

BRYCE: A flock of roustabouts is about the silliest thing I ever heard about.

JULIUS: That we'll see about.

BRYCE: You see a bout?

(A large black bat flies in through the window and hovers over ALICE's bed.)

JULIUS: Is that a bout?

BRYCE: No, it's a bat.

JULIUS: Hereabouts we bat the bat about the roustabouts.

(More and more paper bats drop upon the bed. ALICE sits up screaming.... BRYCE comes to the bed to comfort her.)

BRYCE: Alice, what's the matter?

ALICE: Oh, Jim-Jim...

BRYCE: Shhh! It's all right....

(We can hear the cry of bats from offstage.)

BRYCE: Go back to sleep. It's only a bad dream.... Too many horror movies.

ALICE: Please, Jim-Jim, it's not funny....

BRYCE: I know it's not funny.... Nothing's funny....

ALICE: Why bad dreams all the time?

BRYCE: Too many towns, too many trains...

ALICE: Hand me my medicine... Hand me my medicine...

BRYCE: No.

ALICE: What do mean no?

BRYCE: You're getting too dependent on it. Do you know how much morphine is in this stuff?

ALICE: For Chrissakes, Jimmy, give me my medicine.

BRYCE: Just relax, willya Alice? What's going on with you lately?

ALICE: I've got a doctor's prescription.

(Knock at door)

BRYCE: Yeah. And how many times have you renewed it?

ALICE: None of your business.

BRYCE: It's destructive... What are you trying to destroy yourself for?

ALICE: I just want to sleep...I can't live in this world you're creating for us... It doesn't matter what we do, but you turn it into a routine, and people don't understand it...

(The sound of bats fades quietly away.)

BRYCE: Maybe you want to go back to Hollywood

ALICE: Lay off me, Jim-Jim... Why should I want to go back there?

BRYCE: So you can go back to your Rin-Tin-Tin director.

JULIUS: *(Back in the director's costume)* Somebody call me?

(He crawls into bed with ALICE. BRYCE *exits to bathroom, puts on paper crown.... JULIUS takes ALICE's arm and covers it with kisses)*

JULIUS: Ah, my *cherie*, where have I been all my life.
I look at you and bells sing and birds ring...birds ring?
...Words wing, and the hairs in my nose curl up...

ALICE: *(Aristocratic manner)* Hairs in your nose? Count,
you have no manners?

JULIUS: Manors? I have manors all over the place.
Manors in England, Ireland, and even an estate in
Wales...a whale of a manor My manners aren't fit for
minors...

ALICE: Forget the manners. Let's change the subject
before my husband, the king, gets...

JULIUS: I'm sorry. The king is no subject.

BRYCE: Aha, count, what are you doing in bed with my
wife?

JULIUS: I give up. What am I doing in bed with your
wife?

ALICE: My Lord, you said you'd be out of town this
weekend.

JULIUS: *(Indignantly)* Just what kind of a king are you
not to keep your word? How can the world run if it's
ruled by liars? I hope you're proud of yourself, King
James. It's enough you ruin this young lady's virtuous
reputation by barging in here like this, at this time of
night... What time of night is it?

(A clock chimes three times.)

JULIUS: Midnight... What kind of cad are you coming
home at midnight, waking us up like this? I demand
an apology this instant...I have an appointment for a
nap in the afternoon...

BRYCE: I'm sorry. I didn't realize it was so late....

JULIUS: That's more like it. Come back in the morning
when you can see what we're doing.

BRYCE: Will ten be all right?

JULIUS: Make it ten-thirty...

BRYCE: *(Backing out of his room, closing the door.)* Certainly. Please forgive my rudeness.

(JULIUS leaps out of bed and pulls the curtains off the windows.)

(BRYCE opens the door to the closet.)

BRYCE: Wait a minute. This is my room. What am I doing—being forced, out of my own room? A man's home is his castle.

JULIUS: How do you know this is your room? Do you have curtains on the windows?

BRYCE: Of course I have cur... Where are the curtains on the windows?

JULIUS: Don't get excited. What's your favorite color?

BRYCE: Chocolate mocha yellow...

JULIUS: Then we'll get you chocolate mocha yellow curtains.... Of course furniture will have to match. *(Reaches under the bed and drags out a bucket of red paint. Begins painting a portion of the carpet.)* ...And of course this rug will never do...

BRYCE: Stop it. You're ruining everything.

JULIUS: Quiet. This is the chaos before the creation. You'll just have to get rid of this lamp... *(Takes the lamp and tosses it out the window)* ...See it gives you more room.

BRYCE: How can I see when you threw the lamp out the window?

JULIUS: All you need is more room... Space to spread out in.

BELLHOP: *(Offstage)* Mister Bryce, I have your prescription.

(ALICE and JULIUS turn over the bed. Bedclothes and newspapers get tossed everywhere. The contents of the bureau drawers get emptied all over the floor.)

BRYCE: Maybe you're right... But I hope Clandenberg gets here while there's still something left....

(Just as the frenzied destruction reaches its peak. the BELLHOP appears at the partially opened door.)

BELLHOP: Mister Bryce, I have your prescription...

(He stares in disbelief at BRYCE who has wrapped himself in a plastic shower curtain [which he used as a robe when he played the king], carries a burning newspaper torch, and has a plunger stuck to the top of his balding head.)

BELLHOP: *(Rushes in to put out the flaming torch)* Good God, Mister Bryce, what's going on in here? I'm going to have to report this to the manager... Stop it!

(Lights out immediately)

END OF ACT ONE

ACT TWO

Scene One

(The scene is the same as ACT ONE. *The bed has been righted, and* BRYCE *is back in it. He is talking on the telephone.)*

BRYCE: *(To the hotel manager)* Look, Bernie, it's all a misunderstanding. The doctor told me I needed a little light exercise. It's good for my heart. It's also good for my hair. And so! thought I'd try to redecorate my room. I don't know why everybody's getting so upset about it... For crying out loud, I've been in the same room for the past sixteen years... It needs repainting... All right so you'll send up a painter next week. I may not be alive next week, did you ever think about that? I'll tell you what. Salvador Dali's in town for a self-love festival. Why don't you get him? I'd like a few burning giraffes in the bathroom... Look, Bernie, we've been friends a long time, so there's no hard feeling, huh...I was just fooling around... Look if I wanted your opinions about Salvador's Deli I would have asked you. You think it's all done by paint by number anyway. That's right. I know the guy in Cleveland who runs the factory... He prepares canvases for all the famous painters... Wyeth, Arp, Picasso, Dali-you name them-you don't think they can paint that way without numbers on the canvas, do you? Naah, it's too good. Nobody can paint that good without numbers... That's right. There's a factory in Cleveland that prepares all those canvases...

So that's what I'm going to do for you, Bernie. I'm
going to put numbers on the wall to indicate the colors
I want. One is for brown, two is for guava... Bernie,
you're losing your sense of humor... And another thing
you're surrounding yourself with a staff of prunes. That
new guy who brought me my breakfast... He's a nice
kid but he's got no sense of humor...I'm having a little
fun in my room and off he goes running to you... Why
don't you get the F B I to come up here and spy on me?
Better they spy on me than on our senators... Bernie,
don't hang up on me... I'm warning you, Bernie...
(*Jiggles the receiver*) ...Just for that, Bernie, I'm going to
die in my room just the way D W Griffith did... Your
hotel is going to get the reputation for being a morgue...
(*Dials the manager again, picking up as if he had never left
off*) And another thing, Bernie, you've really let this
hotel go to pot... You've got a lot of nerve complaining
about me moving furniture when I'm afraid to go out
in the hallway because of all the junkies you've got
floating through here... Well, where's Bernie?...
(*Hangs up*)...I don't know why I stay here. The druggist
is taking so much of my money that I can't afford to
stay anywhere else. (*He crawls to the end of the bed and
turns on the television set.*) That's what's killing me.
Crawling back and forth from one end of the bed to the
other. I should get one of those remote control clickers...
(*He looks at the picture, panics, hurriedly changes all the
channels, checks the newspaper television listings.*) ...Those
bastards. They said The Big Store was going to be on
today at three. It's twenty after three now. That's the
trouble with this world. You can't even believe the
television listings... They ought to nominate TV Guide
for fiction of the year award... (*Switches off television,
crawls back to the phone, goes through Yellow Pages, dials*)
...Hello, is this Station 5? Put me through to the
manager... Who is this? I'm one of your dissatisfied
customers. I passed up a lunch with King Gustav to

stay at home and wait for The Big Store to come on television ... What do you mean it was a mistake in the listings? Do you know how much I earn a day? I play half- back for the Los Angeles Rams...I earn more than the President... Our President... Right now I'm supposed to be with my team in the Super Bowl, but I stayed home to watch your movie...I'm going to sue... *(Begins a terrible spell of coughing)* No...I'll be all right... I didn't mean to cough into the receiver... No, lady, you can't spread germs that way. *(He hangs up. He goes over to the breakfast tray where the bowl of cold oatmeal sits. He looks at the alarm clock.)* ...Where the hell is Clandenberg? He tells me he's coming right up. How's he coming? By way of Seattle? What's he care? All I've got to do is sit around and wait for him . Why should I teach him everything I know? Everything I ever learned I learned the hard way *(During the monologue he begins to get dressed again.)* He probably cant even use my stuff. The world is changing. People don't even laugh anymore... Nineteen and he's already sold a script... You make an "X" on paper and people buy it, make a television special out of it What's he going to pay me anyway? Fifteen dollars an hour for me to hand my life's work over to him , and the time he gets through with it, it won't even be my work anymore... Zappo—a life's work up in smoke.

JULIUS: *(Popping his head out)* Zeppo. Is he here?

BRYCE: *(Folds a newspaper neatly and places it under his arm. He is now dressed in his Sunday best.)*

BRYCE: No. I just said, Zappo...it's all over.

JULIUS: What's all over?

BRYCE: Everything's all over. *(Picks up a cigarette lighter)* Zeppo. Zappo. Zippo.

(Lights up on ALICE *who has been sitting quietly upon an upstage chair. She now wears a simple white hospital gown*

over her dress and she sits with her hands folded. From offstage come outdoor sounds—wind blowing, birds, etc. BRYCE walks over to her. He politely removes his panama bat and hands her the newspaper.)

BRYCE: I thought you might like the newspaper.

ALICE: How old is it?

BRYCE: Its this morning's. I bought it for the crossword puzzle, but I left it blank for you. It was quite a temptation, sitting on the bus, staring at those empty squares.

ALICE: *(Not exactly listening)* Shall I have the nurse bring you a chair?

BRYCE: I can sit on the ground. Writing's not like entertaining people. Nobody notices the stains on writers' pants.

ALICE: Back to writing comedy?

BRYCE: I told you last time. Can't you remember? Fun writing for these brothers—fresh from Broadway.

ALICE: They funny?

BRYCE: They're all right.

ALICE: Not like Alice and Jimmy Bryce?

BRYCE: Not like Alice and Jimmy Bryce.

ALICE: Then you are a success.

BRYCE: *(Lights a cigarette)* It's hard to tell. I'm behind the scenes *(Looks at his hand)* Why does my hand shake like that?

ALICE: You didn't bring me any roses.

BRYCE: I was going to.... Honest... It's just that we were up all night working on new routines...Morrie Ryskind's one of these late night guys, and on Sunday all the shops are closed.

ALICE: How's the cactus?

BRYCE: I water it every day.

ALICE: You're not supposed to water a cactus.

BRYCE: I know. Well, pretty soon you'll be dried out and they'll let you out of this place and you can take care of the cactus yourself... Maybe next time I'll remember and bring it to you.

ALICE: I didn't mean to go bananas on you, Jim-Jim...

LOUDSPEAKER: *(From offstage:)* Calling Doctor Quincy Flagstaff... Calling Doctor Quincy Flagstaff... Pick up your tuba at the main desk.

ALICE: I have such bad dreams.

(The BELLHOP *from the previous act passes through the garden, dressed as a hospital orderly. He carries a large telegram [on the same scale as the letters in* ACT ONE*] He doesn't walk through; he comes through on roller skates.)*

ORDERLY: *(On roller skates)* Is there a Captain Jeffrey Spaulding here? Telegram for Captain Jeffrey Spaulding, alias Otis B Driftwood.

ALICE: In one dream I am standing at a huge door, and I open it, and I go down a long corridor, and there is a man in a funny hat standing and staring at me. So I go up and ask him where I am, and he unscrews his legs and hands them to me, and so I start back up the corridor carrying this man's legs with me. The two legs change to one leg, and I go outside where some people are building a house. But as fast as the house is being built on one side, it is being torn down on the other. One man nails up a board and another man comes along and tears it down. So I ask the builder, "Why are you building this house?" and he says, "You need someplace to put your leg so it can dance and dance.

(JULIUS, *carrying a mannequin under his arm, rides through on a bicycle.*)

LOUDSPEAKER: Calling Doctor Hugo Z Hackenbush... Will Doctor Hugo Hackenbush report to the main desk in the main lobby.

ALICE: I was surrounded by people would could remove parts of their bodies... They could unscrew their heads, their arms, their legs... Everything was detached and floating...

ORDERLY: (*Carrying a wooden leg under his arm*) L Cheever Loophole, time for your sedative...

ALICE: I came to you, Jim-Jim...I broke out of here and came running to you and I reached for your hand, and your hand came off, and you walked away, leaving your hand in my hand... It doesn't make any sense.

BRYCE: Maybe it will... Maybe it's not supposed to...

LOUDSPEAKER: Doctor Kornblow, will you kindly remove your bicycle pump from the ladies' restroom...

ALICE: The doctor says that dreams are supposed to tell us something about ourselves...

BRYCE: Ah, doctors. What do they know? Every time I'm at a party I have to explain the jokes to them. They want everything to make sense.

ALICE: But I wake up in the middle of the night... and I ring and ring for the nurse.

(*The phone rings.* BRYCE *gets up to answer it.*)

BRYCE: I don't know. They charge enough. They ought to give decent service. Sanitariums must be run by the same people who run the phone company... (*On the phone*) ...Hello...Clandenberg, where in the hell are you? I've cancelled all my appointments for you...I see. You've been detained but you're on the way up... No. No, it's no bother...I didn't want to lunch with the King of Sweden anyway... last time he got pickle juice all over the place... Yeah, I'm still expecting you...I've been reading through my scripts... *(Hangs up. Returns to* ALICE*)* I have to catch the plane to California, Alice... I'll be back as soon as the script is done...

ALICE: Last time you were gone for two months.

BRYCE: Well, thanks to your director friend, I'm a big success... *(Lights dim on* ALICE.*)*...I'm sorry, Alice, I didn't mean it...

LOUDSPEAKER: Doctor Kornblow, if you don't remove your bicycle pump from the ladies' room this instant, you're going to be sorry!

*(*ORDERLY *enters and starts to take* ALICE *offstage.)*

ALICE: I'll write a letter to our lost cousin...

BRYCE: Lost cousin? Yeah, sure... You do that, Alice. *(He sits on the edge of his bed.*

(A giant gorilla enters through the window and carries ALICE *off.)*

BRYCE:...Bye, Alice... *(A fit of coughing)* Christ, Clandenberg, if you don't get up here soon, I won't have anything to teach you... Some young punk just walks in and takes the best stuff... while I remain behind the scenes... Why should I be waiting for him? He should be waiting for me... Nineteen That's too young to be funny., Besides, in the future, people will just take drugs to make them laugh...

VOICE FROM THE WHIRLWIND: Bryce.

BRYCE: Not again.

VOICE FROM THE WHIRLWIND: Gird up thy loins like a man: for I will demand of thee and answer thou me...

*(*BRYCE *tries to hide under the bed but* JULIUS *pushes him out. He shakes a broom at him.)*

JULIUS: How dare you barge in here without knocking? This is my territory. It's imperative you understand that. That's what's meant by the territorial imperative. (*He ducks back under the bed.*)

VOICE FROM THE WHIRLWIND: Hast thou given the horse strength?

BRYCE: Now that you mentioned it—no.

VOICE FROM THE WHIRLWIND: Bryce, I was merely asking a rhetorical question. I know the answers. Let's take it from the top.

JULIUS: Sam, Bucks, and Rose ought to sign this act up...

VOICE FROM THE WHIRLWIND: Bryce, gird up thy loins like a man...

BRYCE: That's the third time you've asked me that. If my loins were any more girded, I'd be wearing leaded jockey shorts...

VOICE FROM THE WHIRLWIND: Canst thou make him afraid as a grasshopper?

JULIUS: Afraid as a grasshopper? (*To* BRYCE) There are better lines than that in *A Day at the Races.*

BRYCE: (*Leafing through the telephone book*) I don't want to die.

VOICE FROM THE WHIRLWIND: Canst thou draw out Leviathan with a hook?

BRYCE: I don't want to die.

VOICE FROM THE WHIRLWIND: Wilt thou play with him as with a bird?

BRYCE: I don't want to die.

VOICE FROM THE WHIRLWIND: Canst thou fill his skin with barbed irons?

BRYCE: I don't want to die.

VOICE FROM THE WHIRLWIND: Bryce?

BRYCE: I've forgotten what we were talking about.

VOICE FROM THE WHIRLWIND: Make me laugh.

BRYCE: Make you laugh?

VOICE FROM THE WHIRLWIND: You heard me.

BRYCE: But it doesn't make any sense

JULIUS: Just look at his stable of writers. They're all too serious, always predicting disaster, earthquakes, the end of the world—Isaiah, Ezekiel, Malachi—you don't see those guys writing for The Marx Brothers.

BRYCE: *(Steps into a long spotlight)* Why did the chicken...

VOICE FROM THE WHIRLWIND: *(Interrupting)* Heard it.

BRYCE: But I have a new ending

VOICE FROM THE WHIRLWIND: Heard it.

BRYCE: One day the Devil was walking along and he

VOICE FROM THE WHIRLWIND: The what?

BRYCE: The Devil... *(Embarrassed)* ...Oh, forget it...

VOICE FROM THE WHIRLWIND: Good...Let me give you some advice, Bryce, Repeating yourself doesn't make anything clearer.

(Another spot picks up the hospital ORDERLY.*)*

ORDERLY: Your wife is very ill. I think you should be here.

BRYCE: All right. I'm coming

*(*JULIUS *emerges from the other side of the bed. He is dressed as the motion picture director.)*

JULIUS: *(As director)* Where do you think you're going?

BRYCE: I've got to go home. Alice is ill.

JULIUS: *(As Director)* I'm sorry to hear that. Should I get someone to replace you on the script?

BRYCE: I'll mail you the material from New York.

JULIUS: *(As Director)* I've heard that before.

ORDERLY: She wants to learn to play the tuba.

LOUDSPEAKER: Will whoever removed the elevator shaft from the East Ward please put it back immediately?

JULIUS: *(As Director)* Look, I'm sorry about your wife... but you've been running back and forth to the sanitarium for the past six months We've got to have that material.

BRYCE: *(Packing.)* Your depth of concern moves me deeply.

JULIUS: *(As Director)* Who throws in extra money for your train fare?

BRYCE: All right. I'm sorry... What's the rush for the material? Everybody's heard it all before anyway.

JULIUS: *(As Director)* Why don't you bring her out here?

BRYCE: *(Slams the suitcase shut)* Because I don't want her out here.

JULIUS: *(As Director)* You're right. It would probably be awkward to have your wife and your mistress in the same town.

BRYCE: *(Snapping the locks)* What?

JULIUS: *(As Director)* Nothing...

BRYCE: Maybe you just want her to be out here with you.

JULIUS: *(As Director)* Don't push me, Bryce, you're not that talented.

BRYCE: Forget it.

JULIUS: *(As Director)* I'm calling George Kaufman to see if he can take over the script.

BRYCE: *(Heads toward the door with his suitcase. He turns, faces the Director.)* Hast thou given the horse strength? Hast thou clothed his neck with thunder? Canst thou make him afraid as a grasshopper? The glory of his nostrils is terrible.

JULIUS: *(As Director)* What's that?

BRYCE: Just some poetry of mine. I just want you to know what you're trying to replace.

JULIUS *removes the Director's hat and places a chefs white hat on.* BRYCE *sits at desk, places suitcase on lap like table.* JULIUS *enters as Chico.)*

JULIUS: Whatja want for breakfast, boss?

BRYCE: Hominy grits.

JULIUS: As many as you want.

BRYCE: What do you mean as many as I want? I just want some hominy grits.

JULIUS: Look, boss, don't expect me to read your mind. I don't know how many you want.

BRYCE: Not how many... hominy.

JULIUS: Repeating yourself doesn't make anything any clearer... You have the mind of Minnie Mouse.

BRYCE: Minnie Mouse? You have a singular noun with a plural adjective... You mean many mice.

JULIUS: O K, boss... How many mice do you want?

BRYCE: Not mice for breakfast, but hominy grits...grit, grit, grit...what you do with your teeth.

JULIUS: *(Imitating* BRYCE*)* Grit, grit, grit—what you do with your teeth... Here. Have a dish of oatmeal and forget about it.

(He hands BRYCE *the tray of oatmeal that has been sitting on the dresser.)*

BRYCE: *(Stands up, allowing the suitcase and silverware to crash on the floor.)* I don't want oatmeal...I want hominy grits... *(He goes to the window and drops the oatmeal out.)*

JULIUS: Look, just because your wife's been unfaithful—don't take it out on me.

BRYCE: *(Returning center stage)* What did you say?

JULIUS: Forget it—I'll play the Andrews Sisters to settle your nerves.

*(*JULIUS *places a 78 rpm on the antenna of the television set and spins it.)*

BRYCE: *(Opens a drawer and removes a custard pie.)* Why the Andrews Sisters?

JULIUS: Because you're talking about harmony greats all the time

(He places his finger on the record and we hear music.)

BRYCE: Harmony greats *(Hits* JULIUS *in face with a pie)* Not funny...

JULIUS: You're right. It wasn't funny because hitting me with a pie had no context. Also no bananas.

BRYCE: Everything in the world is out of context. Like a bad dream.

JULIUS: *(Wipes some of the pie off and tastes it)* Hmmm. Tastes like hominy grits...

BRYCE: *(With can of whipped cream)* Maybe whipped cream would be funny...

JULIUS: Okey dokey, boss, we try it. Just for that I'm going to drown the cactus.

BRYCE: *(Spraying the furniture)* Let's cover the world with whipped cream and water...

JULIUS: More appetizing than carbon monoxide...

BRYCE: *(Sprays the television set with whipped cream)* Take that Channel 5...that'll teach you to change your schedule.

(Again, just as the mayhem reaches a frenzied peak, the BELLHOP makes his appearance at the partially opened door. He is covered with dried oatmeal.)

BELLHOP: All right, who threw the oatmeal out the goddamned window? *(He stares in disbelief at the strange figure of BRYCE covered with water and whipped cream and then at the furniture dotted with white spray.)* ...Good God, look at this mess... This is it, Mister Bryce.... *(Hysterically)* You're going to get yourself thrown out of here... D W Griffith never acted like this!

(Lights out)

(End of Scene One)

Scene Two

(The room is in shambles. The bed has collapsed. BRYCE is on the mattress on the floor. He leafs through the phone directory again. There has been no attempt to clean up the room.)

BRYCE: Sam, Bucks, and Rose...I must have the only agents in the world who have a unlisted number. No wonder I haven't had any work in the last sixteen years... All the people who want my scripts can't find my agent's number... Oh, my God, why didn't I think of it? All this time they've been going over to the Beverly

Wilshire for me... There's probably a guy named Bryce
registered at the Beverly-Wilshire and he's been raking
in the money all these years.... He's probably famous....
They've been doing my scripts under different names
all this time...I might have written Lawrence of Arabia
and I don't even know it... Some camel probably
walked off with the Academy Award... *(Moving his
finger down a lit of names in the phone directory)* ...Here's
a good name... Polly Potter...Polly want a potter...
(He dials the number.) Hello, is this Miss Polly Potter...
Oh, she isn't at home now... Well, whom do I have
the pleasure of speaking to... Oh, this is her roommate,
Gladys... Well, can I speak to you? ...Who am I? ...I'm
Jimmy Bryce and I used to write for the Marx Brothers...
No, I'm not a close friend... No, I don't know Polly...
I just picked her name out of the phone book... Look,
this isn't an obscene phone call...I'm sick. Listen to my
cough. *(Covering the mouthpiece, he speaks to the audience)*
...Where the hell is my cough, when I need it? Diseases
never come at anyone's convenience. *(He removes
his band and makes several very feeble coughs into the
telephone.)* ...You wouldn't hang up on a dying man,
would you? ...Look, being ill isn't the same as being
obscene... You want me to say something obscene?
All right, you're asking for it... Christ, my mind's gone
blank. I can't think of anything obscene. Give me a
hint... I got it... Gird up your loins like a man... How's
that?...I remember reading that somewhere...I think it
was on a Girl Scouts' calendar... Look, I didn't mean
to say anything against the Girl Scouts...I would have
joined, but they conflicted with my wife's tuba lessons
... Please don't hang up. I'm calling on serious business.
You see Channel 5 was supposed to show *The Big Store*
at three, and it isn't on... What's it to you? Are you
going to let the television stations lie to you and get
away with it? It's time for citizens to rise up... So what
if you've seen *The Big Store*? I want you to call the

station and complain... Repetition's the heart of
comedy... You take a bath every day don't you? No,
you're right. That isn't funny. Can I leave you my
number and maybe Polly can call me when she gets in...
Why not? I don't have anybody else to talk to...It wasn't
very obscene, was it? I don't care what you're wearing...
All right, I take back what I said about the Girl Scouts
girding up their loins...I'm sorry I bothered you. (*Slams
the receiver down*) ...Of all the names in the phone book,
I have to pick the one person yearning for an obscene
phone call... Air pollution is sucking the humor out of
people...or maybe the times are changing.

(BRYCE *gets up and goes to the closet for clothes.* JULIUS *falls
out. He is dressed in an African hunter's uniform, complete
with hat and elephant gun.*)

BRYCE: What were you doing in there? Writing closet
drama?

JULIUS: I was hunting for a pair of pajamas. From
Noah's Ark, a pair of elephants, a pair of geese, a pair
of pajamas... There I was in the dark, as the moon rose
over my traps and the stars tripped over my roses...
No matter... and there is no matter to this... and there
before me was a herd of pajamas... Of course I was
angry they were there before me because I was
supposed to be there before them...

(*Sounds of Africa are heard.*)

JULIUS: And so I leveled with my rifle...I said, "Rifle,
I must be honest with you. I can't shoot the side of a
barn door. I can't even think of a reason to shoot the
side of a barn door."

(*On a black thread, a la shooting gallery style. tops and
bottoms of pajamas pass through the room.*)

JULIUS: So there I was stalking the wild pajama...two of
'em...I stalked, I rooted, I leaved...I raised my butt to my

shoulder...It would rake a contortionist to do any better... The butt was at my shoulder and I fired...

(He fires the gun and a pajama fails to the stage. JULIUS quickly places the rifle in BRYCE hands, leaps back into the closet and closes the door. BRYCE stands dazed clutching the rifle as the BELLHOP enters.)

BELLHOP: Mister Bryce, are you all right?

BRYCE: Huh?

BELLHOP: Did you just fire that gun?

BRYCE: Gun? Yeah. It must have gone off accidentally. my wife and I used it in the act.

BELLHOP: It must have been some act... Here you better let me have it before you do any more damage.

BRYCE: It was some act and then the whole world went bananas... pajamas...something.

BELLHOP: *(Takes the rifle)* Please, Mister Bryce, don't get into any more trouble today... Let me help you clean up in here and then you go to bed... Take the medicine I brought you and go to bed.

BRYCE: You care what happens to me?

BELLHOP: *(Gently, in spite of the oatmeal et al.)* It's Bernie's orders. He wants me to keep you quiet. You're disturbing the rest of the guests.... They're complaining to the manager...

JULIUS: *(Opens the door to the closet, pops his head out.)* No wonder nothing gets painted around here. This room will never get painted with the manager listening to complaints...I want to complain about the manager listening to complaints. *(He closes the door again— jack-in-the-box fashion.)*

BRYCE: Look, kid, I've been at this studio for sixteen years, and they want me to hand my scripts over to some punk...ain't I entitled to some fun?

BELLHOP: Look, you lie down, and Bernie will get somebody to clean this up.

BRYCE: Just because a man is losing his hair, doesn't mean he's an invalid... The trouble with you young punks is that you don't understand the world... Is Bernie going to paint my room before I die? I don't ask much. A little mural here and there...I'll lay it out in paint by number for him.

BELLHOP: *(Picking up newspapers)* He said for me to tell you that you haven't paid the rent in seven months.

BRYCE: Eight months. He can't even count.

BELLHOP: He said seven...

JULIUS: *(Opening the door)* We demand that he charge us for eight *(Looks at* BRYCE*)* ...Why not, it's tax deductible... *(Slams the door shut)*

BRYCE: I'm raising the money. I have a student coming up here. A punk named Clandenberg. I'm giving him some of my funniest routines... But you probably don't know what comedy is... You're the kind who sits at home all day predicting the end of the world.

BELLHOP: *(Ignores the insult)* I'm not a Jehovah's Witness if that's what you mean...

BRYCE: Look, it's not your fault you don't have a sense of humor... You just want to make sense out of everything... You probably think I've gone bananas... shooting off rifles, spraying whipped cream on the television set...

BELLHOP: Dropping oatmeal out the window...

BRYCE: I'm sorry about that. That was an accident. I was standing by the window and I started coughing, and it just dropped out... Look, I'm paying to have your uniform cleaned, aren't I?

BELLHOP: *(Picks up the cactus)* What do you want to do about this cactus? It's dying...It looks as if somebody over-watered it.

BRYCE: *(Gets up)* Put that cactus down!

BELLHOP: *(Puts the cactus down.)* All right...I didn't mean any harm.

BRYCE: *(Picks up the cactus)* Just leave it alone... What do I care if it's dying? It's a keepsake, a memento, that's all... My wife gave it to me.

BELLHOP: You two must have been very sentimental... *(Starts to exit)*

BRYCE: Well, she didn't give it to me exactly... She died and I took it. *(He places it on the window sill so it can catch the last of the late afternoon light.)* ...The citizens of Lincoln, Nebraska, presented it to us for a performance we did there once... What am I telling you for—you don't know the capital of Nebraska.

BELLHOP: Lincoln's the capital of Nebraska, everyone knows that. I'm going down to get a mop.... You better let somebody mop up this room for you.

BRYCE: Let it go. It's my room, ain't it?

BELLHOP: It belongs to the hotel.

BRYCE: I belong to the hotel. You belong to the hotel. Everything belongs to the hotel...

BELLHOP: Some things do. You can't go around shooting holes in the walls.

BRYCE: Why not?

BELLHOP: Because it's against the rules.

BRYCE: You mean somebody actually sat down and made up a rule and wrote it down... People shouldn't shoot holes in their walls?

BELLHOP: I suppose so.

BRYCE: That poor schmuck... Bring me the rule. I want to see the rule.

BELLHOP: I'll tell Bernie...

BRYCE: Hey...

BELLHOP: What?

BRYCE: Do you have a name? Or did you come into this world nameless...

BELLHOP: Call me Gordon...

BRYCE: O K, Gordon, I've written this book of philosophy and its like a math book... It has the questions in the front and all the answers in the back... so if you have a problem, you just turn to the rear of the book for the answers. I'll leave it to you in my will.

BELLHOP: Gee! Thanks, mister. I can't wait.

BRYCE: Jimmy... If you see a kid named Clandenberg down there, send him right up will you, Gordon?

(BELLHOP *starts out.*)

BRYCE: Hey, Gordon!

BELLHOP: What?

BRYCE: I just want to thank you for...for...picking up the papers and stuff...

BELLHOP: We'll add it to the bill...

BRYCE: I wanted you to know.

BELLHOP: Well, it was a toss-up between coming up here or going to Bermuda for the week-end.

BRYCE: Everybody's a comedian!

(BELLHOP *exits.*)

BRYCE: *(Going to the door, calls after the* BELLHOP.*)* I really appreciate you coming up here like this...

(ALICE, *in her red dress, crawls through the window, in her struggle to enter, she knocks the cactus to the floor.*)

ALICE: *(From the window)* It's about time you appreciated me coming to see you like this.

BRYCE: I wasn't talking to you...I was talking to Gordon...

ALICE: Gordon?

BRYCE: The bellhop. Some kid who believes in the rules.

ALICE: I should have known it... When I was born, the doctor patted me on the back—that's the last time anybody pats you on the back for anything in this world... *(Picks up the cactus and replaces it on the sill)* ...See what you did, you big lug-you put the cactus in a place right where somebody could knock it over.

BRYCE: I should have remembered the traffic on the fifth floor sill.

ALICE: It's a good thing cactus is tough.

BRYCE: Lasts longer than roses.

ALICE: That's the thing about a cactus, Jim-Jim... You can place it in the middle of a desert and it grows and grows.

BRYCE: Los Angeles ain't exactly a desert.

ALICE: Been outside lately?

BRYCE: I'm too busy feeding my herd of pajamas.

ALICE: Well, it's crummy. There's even oatmeal all over the street... Here's a letter from Boys Town.

BRYCE: What did you come back for, Alice?

ALICE: I heard there was a good movie on television.

BRYCE: Forget it. There's only serious stuff on. The effects of the Rutabaga on National Defense.

ALICE: Just your luck, .Jim-Jim, for your kind of humor to be taken over by current events.

BRYCE: Maybe it's time for my comeback. We've got a country rife with nostalgia.... Where in the hell is Clandenberg? The kid must have a lot of brains if it takes him all day to get here.

JULIUS: *(Enters from the closet door)* Clandenberg ought to be thrashed to a pulp... But you probably couldn't find a pulp to thrash him to.

ALICE: I told you from the first. If you want success, you've got to push them. People forget unless you keep after them.... You got to do things for them...

BRYCE: Sleep with them maybe.

ALICE: *(Pause. Lights a cigarette)* Maybe.

BRYCE: Well, I have my pride.

ALICE: *(Brings a chair downstage)* Blow.

BRYCE: Handkerchief... Don't get held up.

ALICE: Held up. Belt... Always an excuse. *(She takes pills from a vial and swallows them.)*

BRYCE: You're on the right scent.

ALICE: Cent? Penny...

BRYCE: What excuse?

ALICE: *(Takes out a blindfold)* Pride.

BRYCE: Pried? Screwdriver.

ALICE: How much pride do you think Rin-Tin-Tin had? Look what he ended up with.

BRYCE: Rin-Tin-Tin had more hair than I had....
Take note, Alice.

ALICE: Note-notes. Piano notes. Keys...

BRYCE: You see? My memory system works.

ALICE: Keys... Locks... Locks... Hair... Hair today,
gone tomorrow...

BRYCE: it doesn't work if you don't know where to
stop... That's the trouble with memory. You've got to
know where to stop... Maybe we should sell this system.

JULIUS: Repetition does not make life easier.

ALICE: I just remembered, Jim-Jim. Everything you had,
you gave away.

BRYCE: I suppose I gave you away to that Rin-Tin-Tin
director.

ALICE: *(Sits down, facing the audience)* That was a long
time ago, Jim Jim.

BRYCE: It doesn't make sense,..

ALICE: Cents... Dollars...molars...teeth...it got you your
break, didn't it? ...Success kept coming toward us and
you kept running away from it.

BRYCE: I don't have bad dreams every night.

ALICE: No. You just live them.

BRYCE: Imitate a woman for me, Alice.

(ALICE *ties the blindfold over her eyes.*)

JULIUS: *(Stepping forward amid a fanfare)* As an encore
to their hilarious imitations, Alice and Jimmy Bryce
will now present their world-famous world-fabulous
mind-reading act...

BRYCE: As you can see, my wife is blindfolded. Can you
see anything, Alice?

ALICE: Where is everybody?

BRYCE: Now without any codes of any kind, my wife and I will show you a genuine experiment in thought transference... My wife has radar like a bat and can pick up the most sensitive thoughts... *(Suiting the action to the words)* ...Now I'm going to stroll out into the audience. Now if members of the audience will hold up objects for me... *(He goes to a man who has a watch.)* O K, Alice, let's make this act tick... Let's not talk...

ALICE: *(Repeating the obvious code words)* Tick. Talk... Tick Tock... You are pointing to a watch.

BRYCE: Ladies and Gentlemen, is that not amazing?

BELLHOP: *(Rising as a member of audience.)* Get those people off stage...

BRYCE: *(Holds up a blue handkerchief)* Don't blow this one, Alice.

ALICE: Blow this one... A tuba?

BRYCE: A tuba? Who would bring a tuba to the theater?

ALICE: I thought there was a lady in the front row with a tuba.

BRYCE: No, that was her nephew...anybody knows the difference between a tuba and a nephew...

ALICE: Knows the difference... Nose... Don't blow this... You must be holding up an anteater...

BRYCE: An anteater?

ALICE: Well, you mentioned a nephew and a nephew has aunts. And aunts have blue handkerchiefs.

BELLHOP: *(As a member of the audience)* It's a fake!

BRYCE: *(Holding up a belt)* Let's not get held up with this one!

ALICE: Held up? a gun?

BRYCE: Don't waste time

BELLHOP: I wish I had a gun

ALICE: Held up waist... Suspenders!

BRYCE: Alice, concentrate

LOUDSPEAKER: The Rufus T Firefly Committee on concentrated prune juice is meeting in the Montgomery Ward

BRYCE: The audience pants for your answer.

ALICE: Held up...waist...pants... *(Triumphantly)* ...a belt!

LOUDSPEAKER: Will whoever removed the ladies' restroom from the East Wing please return it immediately?

(BELLHOP *returns to stage, putting on the hospital gown.)*

BRYCE: Ain't it wonderful, ladies and gentlemen, the way second sight can function in our lives.

(ALICE *removes her blindfold and stands up amid the spotlight as* BRYCE *returns to the stage.)*

ORDERLY: I'm telling you, Mister Bryce-your wife will be lucid for a few months, maybe as long as a year, maybe longer. She will function very well, but she will come back here.... It isn't nice, but those, unfortunately, are the facts.

(ALICE *returns upstage and sits on the windowsill.* BRYCE *picks up the battered typewriter, wipes the whipped cream off the keys and begins to type.)*

ALICE: Jim-Jim, did you know that when you're lost in a desert, there's a kind of cactus you can cut open and suck the juice from? It often saves a man from dying of thirst.

BRYCE: Yeah. I know. I learned it from an old western movie I saw at the old Rialto.

JULIUS: The Rialto?

BRYCE: Yeah. I learned to read there. My cousin couldn't read the titles to the silent films and so I read the titles to him. Soon I was reading titles to everyone in the neighborhood. *(Crosses to his desk and picks up the letters from Boys Town)* Soon my cousin got miffed and ran away.

JULIUS: What are you going to do now?

BRYCE: I've decided to answer Boys Town before I die. I don't want to go out of the world owing Spencer Tracy a letter. Let's see. What shall I write about? What's the name of the premier of Burma?

JULIUS: Sounds like a folksy letter.

BRYCE: Who was going to save the world in '62, U know?

JULIUS: *(Answering the question)* U Nu.

BRYCE: I never knew. You know?

JULIUS: Its U Nu, not U no.

BRYCE: It's not what?

JULIUS: It's not what you know, but who you know. Sometimes it helps to know U Nu... Shall we start again...

BRYCE: Oh, no.

JULIUS: Not O. No... U Nu.

BRYCE: Why must I get into these hassles with you? You know?

JULIUS: I know you knew, it's not to Yu, you know, it's to U Nu, you know? You may know I know, but you don't know U Nu.

BRYCE: I'm sorry I started it... Maybe Spencer would rather hear about Charlie Chaplin's wife...

JULIUS: Oona?

VOICE FROM THE WHIRLWIND: Bryce!

JULIUS: Why don't we have Muzak like the other hotels?

VOICE FROM THE WHIRLWIND: Bryce! I know you're there.

BRYCE: All right, I'm here.

VOICE FROM THE WHIRLWIND: Disregard my previous message...

BRYCE: What previous message? ...What previous message? Is anybody there?

(We hear the VOICE FROM THE WHIRLWIND *snoring.)*

BRYCE: What do you think he means by that?

JULIUS: Sh-h-h... He speaks in parables...

BRYCE: Parables?...

JULIUS: Like crossword puzzles. It's a code of sorts.

BRYCE: A code? Like a head code?

JULIUS: Don't worry. I'll break it. I'll figure it out for you. I'm an old hand at breaking codes...codes of honor, head codes, sinuses...

(Lights up on ALICE *seated upon the window sill. The neon signs blink on and off behind her.)*

ALICE: I was at a dinner party, and everybody there was very successful, but when we started to eat, all the silverware was gone, but the people stared straight ahead and didn't say anything, so I folded my napkin and it flew away. I got up to go home, but when I put on my coat-a full-length mink coat-all the silverware fell out and a vase of flowers fell out of the pockets. Everybody accused me of stealing, but I hadn't stolen anything.

JULIUS: Stop the music. I understand it perfectly.

BRYCE: You do?

JULIUS: Certainly. All the objects on the earth, all the objects right here in this room are merely signals; they're spelling out a message in code...

BRYCE: And the message is?

JULIUS: Disregard all my previous messages.

(From offstage we can hear the sound of a tuba being played.)

ORDERLY: You can go in now, Mister Bryce...

ALICE: *(Holds up newspapers)* Jim-Jim,- I've done all the puzzles you've sent me...you see...even the diagramless...I bet you didn't know that *nu* is the thirteenth letter of the Greek alphabet... You can learn all sorts of things doing crossword puzzles.

BRYCE: *(Trying to make a joke)* Nu? No. I didn't know *nu.*

ALICE: Good old Jim-Jim, always full of jokes...I've been memorizing the old routines...

LOUDSPEAKER: Gordon's Committee on the Moral Equivalent of Elevators will meet in the North Tower...

BRYCE: That's good, Alice... But I'm a writer now. I stay behind the scenes. The others take the bows...

ALICE: I hear those brothers are very funny...

BRYCE: That's right. You can't exactly accuse rue of being afraid of success anymore...

ALICE: You don't want to go back on stage no more? You gonna give your best stuff away... Leave the thunder to somebody else?

BRYCE: That's-no thunder, Alice...It's just a bad case of indigestion.

ALICE: Jimmy Bryce's philosophy...

BRYCE: Maybe you're right, Alice, I'm getting tired of putting words in other people's mouths and watching them take the bows.

ALICE: Maybe I did want too much for us...

BRYCE: How can anybody want too much?

ALICE: What are you going to do about me, Jim-Jim?

BRYCE: What do you mean what am I going to do about you? ...I wrote you...Donald MacBride's wife has a house in upstate New York... They want you to stay with them for a while...provided you don't bring the tuba, that is...the country, the fresh air will do you good.

ALICE: Why don't you want me to come to California with you?

BRYCE: The nation's tilted west, Alice... Every screwball ends up in California.... Besides what fun will it be for you to be cooped up in a hotel room while I'm pounding out routines?

ALICE: Jim-Jim, why don't you want me to come to California with you?

BRYCE: You should be near your doctor.... It's his advice...

ALICE: You've found somebody else, haven't you?

BRYCE: No.

ALICE: I've been here a long time.... It's not easy to laugh alone

BRYCE: Since when is that the most important thing?

ALICE: Since when isn't it?

BRYCE: Maybe I'll send for you later...

LOUDSPEAKER: (*Tape made at normal speed, played back at very slow speed.*) Who was tam-p-e-r-in-g w-it-h t-h-e

sp-e-a-ker u-n-i-til Doctor Hu-g-o Ha-c-ken-bush
p-le-ase re-p-o-rt to t-he ma-in d-esk...

BRYCE: Come on. You've got the best medical attention
in the world right here.

LOUDSPEAKER: *(Tape made at normal speed now played
very quickly.)* Quincy Flagstaff, will you kindly pick
up the pregnant kangaroo from the Maternity Ward...

ORDERLY: *(Runs out with artificial wings strapped to his
arm.)* I can fly. I know I can fly...

ALICE: I wish things were different, Jim-Jim...

BRYCE: If wishes were beggars, horses would ride..

ALICE: If beggars were horses, wishes would ride...

ORDERLY: If riders were wishers, beggars would horse...

JULIUS: If wishes were ridden, horses would beg...

(Sounds of a jet plane taking off.)

LOUDSPEAKER: Will the doctor with the artificial wings
who took off on Runway 9 please refrain from strafing
the patients?

ALICE: Then you're not taking me with you.

BRYCE: I think the change will be too difficult.

ALICE: I hope she doesn't go bananas on you, Jim-Jim.

BRYCE: *(Movements, words all go backwards)* difficult too
be will change the think I...

LOUDSPEAKER: Room rest from pump bicycle your
remove kindly you will Kornblow Ronald...

ALICE: Fm getting everything backward...

VOICE FROM THE WHIRLWIND: Message previous
disregard...

BRYCE: Difficult too be will change the think I...

ORDERLY: *(With wings)* Alice, bed to go to time...

ALICE: But the sun just rose; it's time to get up.

ORDERLY: Rules those made who?

ALICE: The sun is coming up, but it's dark.

BRYCE: *(Backs out of the scene)* Bye, Alice...

ORDERLY: Alice, leg your forgot you...

(ORDERLY hands ALICE the artificial leg.)

JULIUS: *(Handing ALICE the bicycle pump)* Pump bicycle...

ORDERLY: *(Removing his wings)* Lady my for wings...

JULIUS: *(Handing her BRYCE's red wig)* Wig red...

ORDERLY: Stick pogo...

(JULIUS and the ORDERLY bring in a strange inventory of objects, reciting the names backwards. They back in and out.)

ALICE: *(Standing on the windowsill)* No... No...I don't want any more of this...Jim-Jim, I can't live in the world you're creating for me.

(The neon sign behind her blinks on and off.)

VOICE FROM THE WHIRLWIND: Man a like loins thy up gird: me thou answer and thee demand will I...

ALICE: Jim-Jim, I don't want to live anymore. *(She turns, her back toward the audience.)* To hell with the tuba!

(ALICE leaps off the sill as the neon sign blinks on and off, an indifferent electric eye.)

BRYCE: I got it.

JULIUS: What?

BRYCE: I figured out the problem with life....

JULIUS: Too many distractions and too much advertising.

BRYCE: No. We grow old too quickly and we work too much. So my solution is to initiate the four-hour day...

JULIUS: No more working eight hours a day?

BRYCE: I mean, The Jimmy Bryce Four Hour Day... one day is four hours long...

JULIUS: *(With castanets, he breaks into a dance.)* An hour for lunch.

BRYCE: An hour for sleep.

JULIUS: An hour for love.

BRYCE: An hour for celebrating Margaret Dumont's birthday.

JULIUS: Mother! But there's a problem.

BRYCE: Mothers are always a problem.

JULIUS: No, with only four hours per day, calendars will be so thick that people will get hernias lifting them.

BRYCE: Why not give every day the same date? See one number and you've seen them all. This passion for statistics doesn't make sense.

JULIUS: *(Counting on his fingers)* A child will be six years old before his first birthday.

BRYCE: Good. No more going broke buying useless presents.

JULIUS: The manufacturers will do everything in their power to keep your plan from going into effect... They'll assassinate you they got a sane way of doing things...

(A bullet is heard to go off. We hear it ricochet.)

JULIUS: Duck. That's the assassins now... They're after you.

VOICE: *(At the door)* All right, Bryce, Jimmy. This is the manufacturer of laugh tracks... Come out with your hands up.

BRYCE: Douse the lights.

(JULIUS takes out a water pistol and douses the lights.)

BRYCE: Look,, you dirty coppers, you guys are going to have to come in and get me. I'm not surrendering the four-hour day.

VOICE: *(At the door)* The four-hour day has been declared illegal.

BRYCE: You guys are against everything but rules... your rules.

VOICE: *(At the door)* Telegram for Bryce, Jimmy.

(Door opens. An unseen hand delivers the telegram— a large bomb wrapped in a red ribbon. A gift card bangs from the ribbon. A long fuse burns ominously.)

BRYCE: Who's it from?

JULIUS: *(Reads the card.)* Gummo.

BRYCE: Gee.

JULIUS: G is for the great gifts Gummo grandly and graciously gives...

BRYCE: G is for the gags that got away. Hold it, there aren't two Gs in Gummo.

JULIUS: You're jealous because you never had two Gs in your entire life.

BRYCE: I had money once, but my wife's doctors got it.

(Timer goes off.)

(JULIUS returns to the door and opens it.)

JULIUS: Avon calling... *(Returns the bomb)* ...Happy Birthday.

(Bomb goes off; the whole building shakes.)

JULIUS: Okey dokey, boss. You sure know the secret to negotiating.

BRYCE: Those guys never were alive.

JULIUS: *(Takes off his mask)* Like the child you never had.

BRYCE: Lay off me, Flammo.

VOICE FROM THE WHIRLWIND: Bryce!

BRYCE: Can't you see I'm busy?

VOICE FROM THE WHIRLWIND: Where was thou when I laid the foundations of the earth?

BRYCE: I can't remember...I was probably at Greenblatt's Delicatessen getting a Cheese Blintz. That's it, you were laying the foundations of the earth and I was ordering a Cheese Blintz

JULIUS: *(Lighting a candle.)* I got it.

BRYCE: What?

JULIUS: I broke the code.

BRYCE: What's it mean?

JULIUS: You remember His message— "Disregard my previous message"?

BRYCE: Remembering's easy... Yeah, I remember...

ORDERLY: She was D O A, Mister Bryce... She leaped from the window and killed herself...

BRYCE: She leave any messages?

ORDERLY: None that we've been able to find.

JULIUS: No, boss, we have to examine the message closely... First of all, he's not used to our language, so he talks funny, He doesn't get the words right all of the time... He doesn't mean *message*... He means *massage*...

BRYCE: Massage?

JULIUS: Now in a massage, you rub oil into something...

BRYCE: Oil?

JULIUS: Take the disregard. That's his accent...
He means in this regard...

BRYCE: *(Goes through the bureau drawers on the floor until he finally comes up with a large gold mask—the mask of comedy)* In this regard...

JULIUS: *Previous... Pre* means the front... *Vious.* he means by us—the V he put in to indicate that it's the fifth floor...

BRYCE & JULIUS: *(Together)* So in this regard by us in the front room on the fifth floor-oil...

JULIUS: That's it. We've got to dig for oil-that's what "Disregard previous message" means... *(Sees the mask of comedy)* What are you going to do with that?

BRYCE: I thought I'd give it to Clandenberg

JULIUS: *(Takes it and turns it around)* Can't you see? It's hollow on the other side. It's not worth anything. It's just one big front Now let's get to work... We've got to get that oil.

(JULIUS and BRYCE run to the closet, break out picks, shovels, and miner's helmets... They begin ripping up the floor...)

BRYCE: Oil! We're going to be rich...I don't have to sell my stuff...I won't have to give to my best routines away... Beautiful black oil, right in my room. Beautiful green money...Isn't it funny how you work for success and it's right in your room all the nine? If Alice had only known...

(As the destruction of the room reaches its frenzied peak, FRANK CLANDENBERG at last appears a: the door. He is a young man of nineteen, neatly dressed in a blue suit.

*He carries a brown suitcase with him, a tennis racket.
And a television script under his arm.)*

FRANK: Excuse me. Is this where Mister James Bryce
lives?

BRYCE: Huh? What do you want?

FRANK: I'm sorry I'm late, Mister Bryce I'm Frank
Clandenberg. We talked on the phone this morning...

BRYCE: Oh, yeah... You're the child prodigy...

(JULIUS exits.)

FRANK: *(Surveying the wreckage)* Am I interrupting
anything?

BRYCE: Oh, no, no I was just remodeling the room
Going to turn it into a school of comedy. *(Notices
the suitcase)* What are you doing with the suitcase?
I thought you were just coming for a lesson...I didn't
ask you to move in with me...

FRANK: Oh this? *(Indicates the suitcase)* ...This is the
reason I'm so late...I got a phone call from New York...
I have to fly there this afternoon , a conference on a new
series.

BRYCE: A new series?

FRANK: That's—what I came over to tell you.

BRYCE: What do you mean you came over to tell me.
I've been By waiting here all day for you. *(Holds up the
mask of comedy.)* I've been going over my scripts and
props

FRANK: I'm sorry, Mister Bryce. I tried to call you a
while ago

BRYCE: What do you mean you tried to call me?

FRANK: The lines were busy Look, let me pay you for
the lesson anyway

BRYCE: No... No. Thanks anyway.

FRANK: (*Picks up the suitcase*) Maybe the next time I'm back in Los Angeles

BRYCE: Yeah, sure Maybe next time (*Looks at the pile of scripts*) Why don't you take some of my scripts with you? Look them over. You can help yourself to the routines. They aren't doing me any good.

FRANK: That's nice of you, Mister Bryce... But my baggage is going to be overweight as it is I sent a trunk to the airport. Why don't you send the scripts to me?

BRYCE: Send them to you?

FRANK: I'm at the Hotel Statler in New York

BRYCE: Hotel Statler

FRANK: (*Fumbles for paper*) Thirty-second Street and Seventh Avenue Want me to write the address down?

BRYCE: Don't bother. I have a good memory.
I remember every drop of moisture in the universe.

FRANK: What?

BRYCE: Just an old joke. (*He tosses his scripts onto the rubble on the floor.*) I'll mail them to you next week.

FRANK: Thanks again, Mister Bryce... (*Exiting*) I'm sorry things didn't work out.

(*The door closes behind him.*)

BRYCE: Sorry it didn't work out... (*Crosses toward the bed*) Send some young punk up here... I wait all day for him, and he doesn't even want the lesson... (*He looks up. His face is a combination of hurt, defiance, and anger.*) "Why did the chicken cross the road?" "Don't mind him, keep your eye on the owl." "To keep his pants up." "That was no lady, that was my wife." ...Alice?... (*He screams*) "To get to the other side." (*With his hands to his head, he collapses onto his bed. He painfully crawls back into position*

*at the head of the bed. He picks up the Mask of Comedy and
turns it over in his hands.)* See, it is hollow on the other
side... That's so you can stick your face into it...

(The phone rings.)

BRYCE: What? *(Starts to answer it immediately, but then
he controls himself. He waits. Then answers it, faking a
feminine voice)* The Beverly-Wilshire... Mister Jimmy
Bryce? ...Just a minute, I'll ring his suites for you...
Suites for the Sweet... *(He makes a feeble imitation of a
phone sound.)* Whom shall I say is calling? Mister Albert
Rose of Gold, Bucks, and Rose? *(He thinks a moment)*
...Mister Bryce is away...digging for oil... He struck it
rich... Hit a gusher... right in his own room! *(Hangs up.
Picks up the receiver again.)* Up yours! *(He can't return the
receiver to the book. The phone falls from the table. We hear
the dial tone)* Imagine The nerve of those guys calling
after all these years They want to make certain that I've
turned everything over to Clandenberg... They don't
care about me... Maybe I should send them ten percent
of my hair... *(He stretches out on the bed.)* . Just keep them
laughing, Clandenberg... That's all *(Almost drifts off,
then rises up)* No. Disregard my previous message...
Go happy... Go sane... Hey, kid, I'm talking to you...
(Collapses back)...I hit a gusher all right... With my luck
I'll probably be reincarnated as a used Bible salesman in
Omaha... *(Pulls the mask of comedy over his face)* ...Lots of
laughs in Omaha... Oma...ha...ha...ha...

(There is a knock at the door.)

BELLHOP: *(Voice)* Mister Bryce. Are you all right?

(No answer from BRYCE.)

*(The door opens slightly. A small area of light from the
hallway spreads across the floor.)*

BELLHOP: *(Voice)* Mister Bryce, are you all right?
I've brought the mops to clean the room.

(Lights out)

END OF PLAY